PETITE PICTURE POEMS

PETITE PICTURE POEMS

Snippets of Life and Whimsy

Linda E. Power

PowerWise Books
New York

PETITE PICTURE POEMS – Snippets of Life and Whimsy, Copyright © 2010 by Linda E. Power. Manufactured in the United States of America. All rights reserved. No part of this publication may be reproduced in any form or by any means, be it mechanical, electronic, photocopying, or otherwise — without prior written permission from the publisher — except for brief quotations in reviews. Published by PowerWise Books, LLC, P.O. Box 162, Putnam Valley, New York 10579. Fax (845) 284-2223. First printing.

This publication is not intended to be a factual account of life or science. Even though some factual information is presented, often fact and fantasy are intertwined to tell an entertaining story. Unless otherwise identified, any resemblance to actual events, people, or places is coincidental. In addition, some poetic license has been taken with word usage and rules of punctuation. This publication is sold with the understanding that neither the author nor publisher is dispensing literary, psychological, or therapeutic advice. The author, publisher, and all others involved in any way with the preparation, publication, sale, or distribution specifically disclaim any responsibility for any financial or personal liability, loss, or risk that may be claimed or incurred as a consequence, directly or indirectly, of the use and application of any of the contents of this book.

ISBN-13. 978-0-9727616-2-8

ISBN-10.   0-9727616-2-4

LCCN 2010902620

Cover Image – Credit and appreciation go to Phoebe Keran for her inspiration and creation of the cover image — at the age of three.

DEDICATED TO
The Limping One, Threezie, and Bumble Bee
And to
The Willing-Hearted

The Limping One, Threezie, and Bumble Bee were three generations of white-tailed deer — mother, daughter, and granddaughter. Each was born, as well as gave birth, in my woods. Each taught her young what she had learned when young. During June, at five-to six-weeks-old, these fawns were brought out of their hiding places at early dawn to briefly frolic in my yard. In time, as they grew more independent, they stayed beyond dawn into the day — curling up and napping in the sunshine.

Bumble Bee was the last generation of this endearing family. Through the seasons, she stopped by frequently and peered into my windows, seemingly inviting me to come out for a chat — possibly with an apple. I awoke suddenly one night in May of 2005 and heard coyotes howling as they do when calling the pack to a meal. I feared for Bumble Bee whose injured leg had never regained full mobility. I have never heard coyotes before or since in the nearby woods — and I have never seen Bumble Bee since. I felt then, as I feel now, that I heard her saying good-bye in the coyotes' howls.

I may have crossed the line with these wild creatures. I did not shoo them out of my yard when they were fawns, and maybe that is why each of them came to me when so seriously injured. I allowed them to sleep in my comfrey patch and eat the leaves to heal their wounds and broken bones, hoping they would regain enough mobility to survive. And I shooed away the bullying deer to protect the injured ones whom I loved — and for five years I was drawn further and further into the "forest." For me it was a time of unimaginable wonder — yet deep, ongoing anguish — a time of raw opening.

The forest is a place where one crosses over — almost without realizing it — yet, allowing it. It is a place of infinite possibilities — not at first apparent. It is where the willing-hearted learn that hearts bewilderingly broken open become hearts evermore open. It is a place where we are called upon, and trust enough, to courageously acquiesce. It is in the shifting shadows of the forest's light-dark play — in the wonders, the losses, and the unknowns — that teach us to move forward as we acquiesce and release to the Divine — that which we are both blessed and challenged to experience.

Many are the forests.

CONTENTS

PART ONE ● LIFE SNIPPETS
Snapshots of Everyday Life — Framed in Admiration, Compassion, and Wonderment

PART TWO • LIGHT LIFE SNIPPETS
Glimpses of Rarely Recognized, Intriguing Energy-Play

PART THREE ● LIGHT WHIMSY
Smile-Inspiring, Fanciful Images — Stirring Wonder

PART FOUR ● WILLING WHIMSY
Picture-Play — Inviting the Inner Child to Freely Romp with Wonder

PART FIVE ● WRITE YOUR OWN
Play with Your Unique Vision

A Book for Willing Hearts — Willing to

●

Enjoy Being Puzzled and Amused
Look Beyond the Apparent
Be Amazed by Simplicity
Broaden Perception
Play with Whimsy
Smile Knowingly
Laugh Readily
Grow Dreams
Make Magic Happen
Acknowledge Miracles
Connect with the Miraculous in Everything

With the Mission of

●

Enhancing Joy
Arousing Wonder
Nurturing Open-Heartedness
Energizing Many-Eyed Vision

PRELUDE

Each Petite Picture Poem is a handful of words intended to create pictures or visual puzzles in readers' minds. The poems are concise by design. When Stanford White, the renowned architect and designer, was questioned about the pricey fee he charged for a plain, yet elegant, magazine cover design, he explained, "The price was for knowing what to leave out."

Petite Picture Poems aspire to connect readers with the miraculous in what appears to be ordinary. Many entries personify nature or mesh reality with fantasy, and flow with fun and mystery into boundless journeys of wonder. More somber entries frame the common human experience in admiration and compassion. Each poem is accompanied by a follow-up comment or short story that complements the poem in some fashion.

To visualize a Petite Picture Poem, simply be open to the amusing, puzzling possibilities and delight in how the pictures may playfully change and perhaps inspire. These little poems are patient companions and will travel at the reader's pace. Longing for return visits, the words may appear to dress anew to inspire fresh, intriguing picture-play.

Petite Picture Poems aim to tickle the mind, touch the heart, and energize many-eyed vision. Readers are invited to wander among the words as if they are puzzle pieces.

Often, after an initial visual comes to mind, another image may surface — possibly with a deeper meaning or different theme. Poems with two themes laid down side by side challenge readers to visualize two pictures simultaneously. Occasionally, a poem will seemingly go in one direction and then appear to embrace an opposite direction — creating a mental optical illusion.

Mental challenges stimulate the brain to evolve further. It is believed by some that Stravinsky's 1913 concert in Paris caused a riot because listeners' brains could not find a pattern in his innovative music. One year later he returned with the same concert and people loved it. Apparently, the brain trains itself to find patterns in the unfamiliar. New experiences eventually generate a flashpoint — a transformative moment — when complacent atoms stir with renewed vitality and suddenly possess new know-how.

To awaken child-essence is to awaken genius. Child-play is the game of being spontaneously in an adventure of endless possibilities. It is said that Albert Einstein's sources of inspiration were largely his imagination and intuition. It is in the state of wonder that dreams incubate — and the innocence of wonder is not analytical. An infant's fingers touching a flower petal do not send messages to the mind asking, "Am I doing this right?" Best yet is that innocence and wisdom are symbiotic traveling companions. One initiates spontaneity and action; the other ushers in evaluation and acceptance.

PART ONE

•

LIFE SNIPPETS

LIFE SNIPPETS

Snapshots of Everyday Life —

Framed in Admiration,

Compassion, and

Wonderment

Eyelids softly curb
A sudden — still formless tear
Life's lens on the heart

A telling tear rarely asks permission to flow into being. It escapes — cloaked in mystery — leaking part of an untold story salted away in the heart for safekeeping.

Sacred meeting places
Duality's fertile edges
Unending meshing

Opposites are fertility-tillers.
They meet, mesh, and merge.
And thus — creation!

See Appendix.

Mud-slide jowls mask
Her set jaw of self-importance
Designer clothes speak

Internal choice-making chisels
from within
our outer facades.

School-bound — in fresh green dress
Dark leather from hip to ankle
Firmly held briefcase

Regardless of your age, pursue your dreams and
carry with you a lot of determination.

Soul-wisdom birthed
Rhythmically through heart channels
Rarely skips a beat

Heart-filtered life experiences often pulsate into
profound, heart-honed wisdom — ever ready to
surface as timely doses of wholehearted consciousness.

Slumbering light
Slips into evening's embrace
Comforting darkness

All that is perceptible involves some other.
And where light meets dark — more than
just the other changes.

Sea of denial
Tiny grains of insight surface
With current ebbing

Have the courage to see what you see —
once it surfaces.

See Appendix.

Hearing her quiet tear
Journey along lash — down cheek
Telling a secret

Listen with all senses.

Bowed mouth — primed

To pierce peace, puncture hope, and wound

With arrogance-arrows

Body language silently — roars.

Living sculptures we are
Wrinkles, eye-shine, body-bend
Hint at our vision

With our perceptions and actions — we continually
sculpt ourselves.

Pink, bow-tied hair ribbon

Worn ends — brush her preteen brow

Loosening threads — dangle

The pink of innocence, eventually, fades and frays into the next phase of the journey.

Young belles — dressed up
Sweet-coated Chiclet-chatter
Air-filled, fading scents

Beneath the apparent superficiality and pretentiousness of youth, rest the seeds intended to germinate into grace and wisdom.

See Appendix.

Caterpillar fuzz

Fans out — as butterfly wings

Warming a willing heart

Life transformations summon us to venture within,
become insightful, release the old, rearrange the
familiar — and be open to embracing the
opportunities that come with change.

Dignified, black-clad wasp
"Why abandon flight to walk?
Looking for something?"

There are always reasons — and choices.

Go at your pace in your fashion to arrive at
your goal. Finding what you are looking for slowly,
step by step, is fine.

Flower-bed intruder
Weed in perfect bloom
Wild integrity

Dare to be who you are meant to be.

And if that is different from the norm, dare to be different. Your splendor will be all the more striking.

Watchful waiting
Intent on witnessing the bud
Burst into bloom

Watchful-waiting phases play with our imagination and test our patience, yet fuel our focus and resolve.

If ever in doubt about realizing your dreams, have faith that you are probably exactly in the place along your path where you are meant to be — and, most likely, further along than it feels.

Autumn dew-droplets
Crystal seeds of timely death
Gently determined

There is a natural order — with an inherent wisdom.

*Autumn wins you best by . . . its mute appeal to sympathy
for its decay.*

— Robert Browning (1812–1889)
English Poet

Her fragile fingers trace

Etched facial lines — telling

Lost-gone-time stories

Read the lines.
Listen to the stories.
Connect with the journeys.
Chart your course.

Uneven dress hem

Wobble-walk in faded flowers

Stitches in life's fabric

Life's journey through nature's cycles is personally varied, yet universal.

Forms shift, strides adjust, flowers fade, pain provokes.

Nurture an inner light and blossom an internal garden of gratitude. And when necessary — mend its demanding outer shell as best you can.

See Appendix.

Invisible wall
Holding her back — covered with
Life's graffiti

How we speak to ourselves can create a wall of
perceptions holding us back — entrapping us
within self-imposed illusions.

All that we are is the result of what we have thought.
The mind is everything. What we think, we become.

— Buddha

Plaid-proper lady
Life of fashioned passion
Seeping out at the seams

Does your persona-wrap suit who you have
become — or are becoming — or wish to be
— or so long to be?

*The personal life deeply lived always expands into
truths beyond itself.*

— Anaïs Nin (1903–1977)
American Author

See Appendix.

Birds-to-fish-to-birds
Interwoven Escher lines
Options — always options

Lines — verbal, visual, physical.

Hear them, see them, feel them — from countless perspectives.

Shift them, sift them — shake out the intriguing possibilities.

He who wonders discovers that this in itself is wonder.
— Maurits C. Escher (1898–1972)
Dutch Artist / Printmaker

Perceive it — become it
Be as an apple blossom
Create an orchard

Perception is our internal, as well as eternal, playground.

We can be as hungry worms gnawing within the apple, or we can be blossoms high on the tree surrounded by the enticing fragrance of like-minded travelers and visited by fuzzy honeybees, lovingly tickling us into fulfilling our potential to flourish.

Choices — always choices.

Day's playful clouds curl up
In sunset's glow — to rest
On Mother Earth's bosom

As passing wisps of form, energized by the sun and supported by the Earth Mother, let us be reminded to start and end each fleeting day with boundless gratitude.

Statistically, the probability of any one of us being here is so small that you'd think the mere fact of existing would keep us all in a contented dazzlement of surprise.

— Lewis Thomas (1913–1993)
Physician / Etymologist / Essayist / Educator
Source: *The Lives of a Cell: Notes of a Biology Watcher*

Her textured face
Thread-worn tapestry of time
Woof of joy — warp of woe

Life's challenges and opportunities continually
summon us — as weavers.

Our warped fiber — heritage, traditions, instilled
beliefs — has been set up and calls us to enhance it by
weaving in the hues and textures of life's experiences.

Positive woofing is often reflected in a weaver's
face as spirited lines of joy, crisscrossing nondescript,
passive contours.

Note: *Warp* threads extend lengthwise on a loom and *woof*
threads (also called *weft*) are woven crosswise through the
warp.

See Appendix.

Years of tears — bursting

Cataracts of denial

Drowning his eyes in pain

A longtime-but-lost friend may come to you in a dream with his eyes engorged with tears of pain for past wrong-way choices and actions. Those tears may have been rushing to the surface for years, wearing down self-righteousness and sharp-edged defensiveness.

Dreams reach beyond the confines of time and place — beyond the you — beyond the me. Tears may act as messengers connecting us to all that is — even when it appears not to have been.

See Appendix.

Maiden Spring's Promise melts
Grandfather Winter's icy stares
And frozen tears

The Promise is eternal.

Warmth unnerves iciness.
Growth nudges aside stagnation.
Joy scatters weariness to the winds.
Calmness leads turmoil away by the hand.
And
Acceptance of the eternal rhythm nurtures resilience
to endure and thrive throughout life's seasons.

Mockingbird antics
Song-filled aerial-dancing
Crazy from the heart

To attract a mate, a male northern mockingbird sang
and sang from the top of a neighbor's TV antenna
while periodically jumping up and landing again on his
perch. Each enthusiastic display lasted more than an
hour. My retired, wheelchair-bound father watched
with such joy at the love-seeking bird's comedic zest
for life.

After my Dad's cataracts took his sight, upon
hearing the mockingbird's song he would ask, "Is he
jumping from the aerial?" I would say "Yes," and my
father would smile from the heart. Those two were
linked by their joy and love for life.

Now, whenever I hear a mockingbird sing I feel
my father's joy, see his smile, and am connected to all
that is dear in life. Honor your cherished memories
and those who co-created them.

Cloud-born — summit-bound
Streamed-rushed — ocean-embraced
Ancient Traveler

As an Ancient Traveler, water fell and flowed,
dissolving and gathering the necessary nutrients
for life. And as the Sower of Life, water carried
and delivered its wisdom into the oceans.

*The ocean is where the first speck of life emerged some
3.8 billion years ago. The speck evolved into algae
capable of photosynthesis, resulting in the first supply
of oxygen. The oxygen, interacting with ultra-violet
rays from the sun, encased the earth in a protective
vale called the ozone layer.*

— Dr. Masaru Emoto (1943–)
Author / Source: *The Hidden Messages in Water*

Face-filled telling-lines
Life stories in reverse braille
Summarizing-smiles

Meander over the faces, follow the lines, be touched
by the stories, and honor the storytellers. Respond
engagingly, "Were you really a race-car driver in the
late '40s?" And witness the delight in her smile as she
nods yes.

Lean in and feel the depth of her love for her
father who never returned from the war. Yet, stay

alert for signs of sweet surprises surfacing in her smile. Maybe, as a child she delighted in eating spaghetti strand by strand because it was fun, and it lasted longer, and it made her little brother squirm and giggle. Maybe, how as a young mother she creatively stretched the budget during the lean times. Maybe, that she still experiences such joy by believing in the essence of Kriss Kringle.

Her smiles are likely to tie together her most cherished life themes. There may be many; there may be few.

Crossing back over

The murky, mucky moat of

Misunderstanding

We can choose to shift perspective and smooth out an unease as soon as we sense a rippling.

We can choose to sift through words and use them respectfully and compassionately.

We can choose to forgive silently and move beyond without trying to justify a position.

In so doing, we can choose to avoid contributing to a debris-ridden, dark abyss, over which we may be required to navigate to reconnect caringly with an alienated loved one.

Shifting — sifting — forgiving — loving — yes!

Autumn's time-blizzard

Leaves — like life's moments — whirl

Into winter's stillness

As we grow older, time seems to whirl by faster —
yet, each moment may be more treasured.

On February 14, 2001, an article appeared in
a local newspaper, *The Daily Messenger*, entitled
"A Seventy-Five-Year Romance." It imparted some
facts about a couple who were celebrating their 81st
Valentine's Day together.

George Power and Frances Canfield started
dating in their high school years while attending
Canandaigua Academy. They graduated in 1922 and
four years later were married. On February 20, 2001,
George and Frances celebrated their 75th wedding
anniversary.

Hearty chickadee-charm
Black cap, gray suit, white vest
Buoyant, heart-honed notes

In reality, the black-capped chickadee's joyful chirping-chatter is a highly complex, language-like communication system with more than a dozen distinct calls.

In addition to excellent communication skills, chickadees have outstanding memories. Storing thousands of insects and seeds for later retrieval, each in a separate spot, chickadees can remember the locations of these food items for up to twenty-eight days.

Weighing only one-third to one-half ounce, the little chickadee packs a lot of enchantment.

Bowed legs — hers and his
Many miles of walk-talk
Sixty-years entwined

Take the time to share and wander with those
you cherish and love.

Grow old along with me
Two branches of one tree
Face the setting sun
When the day is done
— John Lennon (1940–1980)
Singer / Songwriter / Musician

Long-wrong-love lingers
Awareness-tears cascade into
Fog-filled denial

Choice-making inevitably demands that we become
intimately acquainted with life's light-dark puzzle
pieces — especially, joy and sorrow.

Joy and sorrow are inseparable . . . together they come
and when one sits alone with you . . . remember that
the other is asleep upon your bed.

— Kahlil Gibran (1883–1931)
Philosophical Essayist / Novelist / Poet

Heaven-hung hawk
Motionless wings ride airflow
Dart-sharp sight pinpoints brunch

With heaven-ordained roles, all creatures are designed to live in balance.

Hawks, as well as eagles, hunt during the day rather than at night. It is believed that hawks' eyesight is up to eight times more powerful than that of humans and that the golden eagle can spot a rabbit while flying as much as a mile high in the sky.

The bird hunting a locust is unaware of the hawk hunting him.

— Proverb

Shuffling feet pause
Yet, her soul soars buoyantly
On forever-breezes

When an eighty-year-old woman, climbing the stairs
to her 11th floor apartment, was asked how she was
managing after hurricane Wilma had knocked out the
electricity for days — she paused and softly, yet
knowingly, smiled and said, "Grace glides on damaged
feet."

Note: News reported on October 26, 2005.

Out-of-the-nest day
Rudderless chic — heart-propelled
In floundering flight

Nest-leaving invites floundering — and floundering inspires nest-leaving. The two partner in a continual process.

It is meant that we leave nests throughout our lives. And with each flounder we hone our innate skills — preparing for our next out-of-the-nest leap.

Dew-covered rosebud
Cheered by dawn's sun rays
Warms to blossoming

During dark, cold times our true essence and beauty may be shut within.

Being touched by warmth can help burst the bounds of doubt — empowering us to emerge and fill the special places in the world waiting for us.

Be open to the warmth — and be opened by it.

Grandfather Winter
Remembering young love
Melts into Spring's arms

Thawing and flowing into renewal's embrace may be
aroused in ever so many ways — a memory, a scent,
a bird's song, a smile, a note of laughter, a dream, a
touch . . .

Tale-telling lines traverse
Her lacelike face — shining light
On life's shadow-times

Signs of well-worn wisdom are likely to travel
discerningly along cheek and brow lines, or twinkle
suddenly from tranquil eyes, or be revealed subtly
with a slight uplifting of the corners of the mouth
into a serene, knowing smile — all expressing:
"Befriend gratitude and grace as reliable traveling
companions."

Fistful of lollipops
"It's my job till my check comes in."
Said wheelchaired vendor

The telling of life stories can begin with the smallest of
gestures. The most recent chapter may begin when a
sensation of sweetness, or sourness, or intrigue attracts
our attention. Then we tumble backwards through the
yet unknown.

Old woman — old man
One sews; one hoes — hoping to
Finish at the same time

Be reverent of the purity and power of love.
Marvel at the simple ways it can be conveyed.
Share your life. Savor the moments.

Turning and startling
My shadow — we laughed as
We walked along

Certainly, the reverse is more common — being
surprised by our "shadow" — by murky, personal
shadow-traits that slink into our inner light and
are, thus, transmuted.

Sunburn-snow — reflecting
Cold, crystal light-carriers
Fleeting — yet lasting

Robust opposites reflect truths.
In essence, we are all reflections — reflecting.

Black-duck sentences
On bay's autumn horizon
Thank-you notes in flight

Buoyant messages are everywhere — in many disguises.
Yet, they rarely veil their spirit-sparked joy.

Flawlessly fated
Forever flowing and ebbing
Love sculpts and buffs hearts

Fated love is destined to challenge, yet comfort.
It chisels, yet buffs, just enough to bring to light
precious treasure.

Widow Wall's one tear
Amplifying silent love notes
Spills into his grave

Some of our most beloved stories seep through
impenetrable facades and are concisely divulged
in a most down-to-earth manner.

Friday's long blonde hair
Wednesday's shampoo — past due
Frolics as does child

Fortunate are those who are children at play in their
hearts and, thus, unconsciously schedule joy into
their lives.

Sand-grain cousins honor
Grand, time-tossed, sea-tumbled,
Rock-solid forbearers

Each of us is a tiny, yet integral, speck of immeasurable
value to the whole.

See Appendix.

Buds hold secrets

Late-bloomers bear long-held secrets

Bloom — and set secrets free

Some secrets are sweet. Others are less so.

But bloom we must.

Bus-stop-bench waiting
Bent man — long white hair weighing
Knitting his winter scarf

All arrives when it is meant to.
Show up and do your part.

Clasped in heartache
Callous-wrapped, gentle hands
Unfold to tear's touch

Shapers of life are hearts and hands.
Be the loving behind the doing.

PART TWO

•

LIGHT LIFE SNIPPETS

LIGHT LIFE SNIPPETS

Glimpses of Rarely Recognized,

Intriguing Energy-Play

Our cat's whiskers speak
Dust words — cobweb comments
"Clean the summer house!"

Be perceptive,
willing to acknowledge suggestions,
and open to accepting help when necessary.

In dark times — stand tall

As does the sunflower during

A solar eclipse

Faith, held firmly during the dark times, meets again
the light.

Having sunflower-faith during the darkness puts
us where we need to be — to draw to us the light
when it returns.

Which is more amazed?

The unfolding blossom — or

The releasing bud?

We are at the same time the bud and the blossom,
embracing challenges and opening to opportunities.

As the transient bud and its birthing blossom,
we are simultaneously fading and becoming — and
being — always being.

Silhouetted ghost tree
Bare, stubbed limbs — still reaching
Haunting — or wanting?

The unknown invites us to connect with the possibilities.

Enjoy looking beyond the apparent and engaging with ambiguity.

Twilight silhouettes
Breeze-nuzzled autumn leaves
Mime good-bye waves

The Winds of Time touch and teach us all.

The Autumn Wind brings unwavering messages about releasing and acquiescing.

At low tide — walk the flats
Agitate an oyster
Co-create a pearl

Be pearl-energy —
evocatively inspired, yet ever-polished —
core-complete, yet ever-surfacing.

Moth-white-crowned, bent wisp
Market-bound — heart-propelled in
Cardinal-red shoes

We all go to market.
Wear fitting shoes for the journey.

See Appendix.

"Morning, Mr. Fry!"
Passing girl's soft yell — airborne
Old Mr. Fry — mourning

We are all at some place in the eternal-day.

Love strokes, love notes
Softly brushed on his cheek
Eyelash-lustings

Eyelash-language is an expressive art form
— full of close encounters.

Ocean orchestra
Winds, reeds, percussion rocks
Moon-directed score

There is a natural tempo and harmony —
with a multitude of players.

Mother Maple sighs
As wind-whirled, ground-bound offspring
Leave her outstretched arms

Nurturing and budding require letting go —
when the leaving-time comes.

From the muck — with pluck
A princely leap — up from frogdom
To lily-pad standing

*If one is lucky, a solitary fantasy can totally
transform one million realities.*

— Maya Angelou (1928–)
American Poet / Author / Educator / Civil Rights Activist

Tulips on tiptoe
Dew-washed, sunrise-ready
Petals — child-cheek-smooth

Serenely feel a blossom's will to be. And caringly
awaken and nurture such radiant essence within.

Dark, damp earthworm-work
Priming Mother Earth's womb for
Quiet miracles

Well-intended efforts have intrinsic worth — whether
they are recognized by others or not. Be heart-guided
and play a role in creating mini-miracles.

Slant-angle sun rays
Dress slim marsh-grass silhouettes
With silvern evening clothes

Every now and then enjoy being a silhouette in
twilight, adorning yourself in starlight — feeling
your stardom.

Tiny raindrops carry

Rosebuds, oak trees, muddy feet,

Frowns, smiles, hopes — and more

Raindrops beget — and beget. The life-expanding
potential packaged within each bead of water is
miracle-amazing.

With elvish eloquence
Breeze-tossed summer sunbeams
Frolic — giggle — and flirt

Marvel at the mystery of how life at times tosses us
around just enough — to enable our light to bring
out our shadow just enough — to reveal a not-yet-
exposed aspect of our multifaceted selves.

Lonely, barren twigs
After icy months of longing
Weep into blossom

Divine love-energy rides a fluid flow — rippling and
rushing to and through yearnings and longings, twigs
and blossoms, roses and rabbits, groundhogs and
grasshoppers, and you and me — to those yet to be.

Birthday candles beckon
Hopes float to the Wish Giver
On fated smoke-trails

The act of celebrating helps to kindle hope and new possibilities.

Breathing your wishes into a ceremonial flame may convert those desires into a wise energy that knowingly travels on trails of smoke to the Wish Giver. The flame, your wishes, and you as the wish maker are all positively transformed.

Divine Light — gently
Filtered through angels' wings
Lifts a heavy heart

You are always connected to the Light. Look for the signs.

Be heartened by the occasional flickering shadows you may see out of the corner of your eye. Possibly, you will catch a glimpse of an angel's fluttering wing.

Allow yourself to wonder.

Bashful beads of dew — glide
Along spun webs of wonder
Cuddling sunbeams

Slithering along newly spun silken strands, partners
in creation briefly embrace and are forever changed.

Let's create personal, transformative webs of
wonder, along which we travel as beads of life,
embracing the light, glistening and gliding into
encounters and beyond — ever-renewing.

At the corner of

His smile — she takes a turn

Into paradise

Smiles are like bows — they tie things together.

*I love smiles. . . . If we want a genuine smile, then first
we must produce the basis for a smile to come.*

— 14th Dalai Lama (1935–)
Tibetan Buddhist Spiritual Leader and Statesman

Autumn tapestry
Silver-screen threads interweave
Window-framed hues

Nature is an infinite and changing art gallery
surrounding us, as well as reframing itself
continually — at our windows.

Nature is not only what is visible to the eye . . .
it also shows the inner images of the soul . . .
the images on the back side of the eyes.

— Edvard Munch (1863–1944)
Norwegian Painter / Printmaker

Shadow-birds sliding south
Along lofty beach dunes
Jar loose tumbling sand grains

Imagine for a moment that everything is connected to all that is, to all that was, and to all that will be.

Could the tumbling loose of one sand grain, touched by the shadow of a bird in flight, displace enough air to change that bird's migration in some way?

Could the tumbling loose of one sand grain — somewhere — at some time — have contributed to the fall of an empire in another place — at another time?

Sun-graced beach break
Silver-shiny, smooth — driftwood
Speaks of its journey

Although leafless and no longer living as a tree,
driftwood is implicitly linked to the rhythm of life.
It is rocked by the predictable pulse of the tides, is
cradled on Mother Earth's bosom between journeys,
and glistens as it reflects star-shine.

Let it remind us that threads of energy connect
us all. Our journeys and stories — enduring life's ebb
and flow — are entwined. We all reflect some of who
we are, as well as where we have been. And we all need
to be still and rest on occasion.

Fluttering shadow
Skims sunbather's pale body
Butterfly-connection

Be alert to butterfly-messages as they flutter by.
Being tagged by a butterfly's shadow, especially while
preoccupied with skin-deep beauty, is a blessing —
nudging us to look inward to develop a deeper,
unseen beauty.

The varied, multihued inner wings we nurture
and spread are distinctively designed to lift us into
expressive flight and along our true journey.

Dream butterfly-dreams — and awaken to
butterfly-potential.

Heaven-sent life beads
Cleanse, nurture, arouse, renew
Water wisdom

Divine intelligence is everywhere. Marvel at its genius.

And the force that created life and allowed life to evolve was, of course, water. Water was able to do this because it has the unique ability to dissolve the required nutrients for life and carry them from the mountains and rivers into the oceans.

In the process of falling to the earth, seeping into the ground, and then emerging, water obtains information from various minerals and becomes "wise."

— Dr. Masaru Emoto (1943–)
Author / Source: *The Hidden Messages in Water*

Roof-perched raven
Sips from clogged gutter
Of old couple's home

The Spirits come for us in many forms. There are signs
and the timing is impeccable. Life is a wondrous gift.
Returning to spirit is also a gift. In our physical form,
we are not likely to remember the spirit realm from
which we came. Maybe that is the challenge — trying
to remember. On the other hand, maybe the real
challenge is having faith in the unremembered.

In *The Republic*, Plato's version of the Myth of
Er describes how souls preparing for their journeys
to Earth are taken to the Plain of Forgetfulness and
instructed to drink from the River of Unmindfulness.
In so doing, they forget all that had previously
transpired in the spirit world and descend into physical
life on Planet Earth with no memory of their spirit
experience.

Jump-start chin dimple
Yarn-spun laughter lines — looming
Life-fiber-vibrant

Let's explore two possible themes laid down side by side, yet intertwining. One theme appears to focus on facial characteristics; the other seems to relate to a zest for life. The two themes feel as if they interlink through storytelling.

As with an optical illusion, try to picture at the same time both themes as visuals.

Let's play with the words:

- *chin = jaw chin* OR *to speak* (possibly storytelling)
- *yarn = thread-like* OR *story*
- *looming = emerging* OR as a noun = *loom* (machine for weaving) stretched into a verb = *looming* (as related to weaving)
- *fiber = thread, yarn* (for weaving) OR *yarn* (story) OR *character, integrity*

Milkweed seed debut
Floating in fluffy tutu
Looking for booking

In downy white fluff, milkweed seeds dance on
air currents before putting down roots. All to the
applause of the monarchs!

Monarch butterflies need milkweed plants to
survive. They lay their eggs on the underside of the
milkweed leaves. As the caterpillars grow, they eat
the leaves which, by the way, contain poisonous
chemicals. These toxins do not hurt the caterpillar or
the butterfly-yet-to-be — but do make them
poisonous to some predators.

Maybe this knowing — this inner strength —
is the reason why fragile monarch butterflies can dare
to be so colorful.

Stone walls lacing dense woods
Pulsate with handprints and heartbeats
Of long-gone dreamers

And in the country, on hot summer evenings, thunder
vibrates centuries-old fieldstone walls, stirring stories
— not quite audible, yet felt — sensed in the echoes
like heartbeats of the ages — reaching back to the
times before the separate stones were amassed into
defining lines — marking the here from there.

And being stirred by those vibrations, we might
sense a hint of feeling that we are again one with all —
as it was in the beginning — and yet, continues to be.

Touch a rock — and in so doing — touch the
Universe.

Tail-twisting night work

Empress Spider — awaits brunch guests

In webbed wonder

Spiders are supreme masters of spinning, design, and construction. They have special glands that produce various types of silk, each used for a distinct purpose. They push the liquid silk through organs called "spinnerets" located on their abdomens. The silken threads dry as they touch the air. Some varieties of spider silk are so strong they are believed to be as much as five times stronger than an equal amount of steel.

Perpetually beguiling is the miracle-might of nature.

Scripted image-play
Wandering wonder-words
Dream-speak with Spirits

During our night dreams, the unconscious awakens
as teaching images — imparting veiled wisdom and
rebirthing us into creative tomorrows. Dream-sleep
images are captivating communicators.

Occasionally, however, a compelling spoken
message may come through, from behind the scenes,
without being portrayed visually. It is said that these
words and phrases come directly from the Wise Ones
and are profoundly pertinent to the dreamer's well-
being and evolution.

Aloof persona
Softly cloaked in silence
Conceals sweet mysteries

Beyond an apparent façade — in the quiet —
in the not-yet-visible — many treasures may
be waiting.

*"What makes the desert beautiful," said the little
prince, "is that somewhere it hides a well. . . ."*
— Antoine de Saint-Exupéry (1900–1944)
Writer / Aviator / Source: *The Little Prince*

Divine love abounds

In wind-whispers, blossom-smiles

And sunbeam-hugs

Nurture yourself and feed the divine spark within you.

    Strengthen your connection to the divine everywhere — in everyone — and in everything.

You are a distinct portion of the essence of God in yourself.

> — Epictetus (c.55–c.135)
> Emancipated Slave / Greek Philosopher

Thunder fiercely applauds
Piercing lightning darts — threatening
A summer heat wave

Following spontaneous displays of extremes —
light piercing dark,
clamor cracking silence,
uproar trouncing tranquility,
cool currents ousting hot stillness,
thrill bouncing between fear and wonder —
nature calmly composes herself and ushers in equilibrium.

Bright sunbeams — dim shadows
Coupled in light-dark frolic
Both flourish — both fade

Lively, space-traveling sunbeams and sedate, stay-at-home shadows have been faithful companions for ages.

Sunbeams travel about 93 million miles at a speed of roughly 186,000 miles per second to reach earth to brighten each day and frolic with shadows. In contrast, shadows do not travel far at all, but they faithfully show up to greet arriving sunbeams.

Caterpillar dreams
And butterfly blues fuse — while
Struggling cocoon-free

In time, the comfortable cocoon of the caterpillar
becomes a prison for the butterfly. The demanding
struggle a butterfly must go through to free itself
from the cocoon is nature's way of forcing fluid to
flow from the butterfly's body into its wings — fully
forming them for flight.

Meet the challenges — make magic happen.

Alluring marsh grasses
Wave willing sea breezes into
Fleeting caresses

It is a wonder. Which minuscule movement gives birth to momentum? Does one essential energy need to be more influential?

Does willingness lie dormant until sparked by allure — or does allure awaken to the apparent presence of willingness?

Straight, somber ash tree
Sun-bleached skeleton — aglow
With star-shine blossoms

All is starlight in some form — from the soaking-
up-sunshine-and-becoming phase — to the
reflecting-star-shine-and-being phase.

Past, present, future — entwined and aglow.

Brisk breezes inspire dance
Autumn-hued oak leaves twirl
Carefree cloud-partners

In youth, we long for someone to grow old with. In old age, we long for someone to grow young with.

Dance with another in the moment — and it will always be so.

Peaks pierce the heavens

Sipping sacred secrets

Timeless mountain-knowings

Go to the Mountain. Be opened by its pervasive presence — and open to its enduring bonds.

And in the stillness, serenely and deeply — breathe in ageless wisdom.

Today is your day! Your mountain is waiting. So . . . get on your way.

— Theodor Seuss Geisel / Dr. Seuss (1904–1991)
American Writer / Cartoonist

Old Lady Maple
Draped in flowery lace
Still stirring it up

Explore your heart for lace-veiled yearnings. Sift
through and contemplate what you most desire to
do. The discovery may delight you and, ultimately,
someone else.

Butterfly-valor
Turtle-fortitude, hawk-focus
Break through, persist, soar

Break through — and expand into spirited magnificence.
Persist — and remain resolutely journey-focused.
Soar — and explore with perceptiveness.

The Wanderer strolls
Lovingly through time and space
Kindling heart-glow

Be a Wanderer — connected to the divine essence in all. Be rooted in the endless moment — witnessing miracles. Be delight and light — radiating evermore.

The moon doesn't mind
Which insects sing in its light
And which ones do not

Sing when you wish; remain silent when it fits
your needs. The Light shines on you, regardless.

Pulsating ambience
Polar bears and hummingbirds
Entwined heartbeats

To the universal heartbeat, all contribute.
By its collective rhythm, all are interlinked.

White moth — red cardinal

Life-death dance — heartbeat rhythm

To fly away as one

Participate in life's dance, practice the footwork,
twirl to the tempo — and be connected.

Steamy tea-leaf ghosts
Conspire with ready sunrise rays
Brewing a wake-up

Each wake-up may feel rather like an illusion.
And held within the magic is the age-old
wisdom that we are creating it all.

Morning whiskers meet

Aftershave-scented kitty

Sends her master to work

The sweetness of some good-byes
lingers long after the leave-taking.

Fading leaf motif
Air-brushed, yellow-red good-byes
Gusty blue-sky greetings

Autumn's gusty leaving majestically teaches
release-and-accept lessons.

Late-day sunbeams beguile
Staunch fir needles to adorn
Shimmering sequins

Embrace the light and get sparkly sometimes.

Squealing spiders scatter
Cobwebbed cat whiskers — wear
Trophies of the chase

Much of the fun of the game is in the anticipation.

Fog-wrapped sunbeams
Heaven's light seeping into
Phantom mist-beings

Light — both elucidates and mystifies illusion.

On a star-sprinkle night
A brimful moon spills into
Pathways and open hearts

Somewhere, something incredible is waiting to be known.

— Carl Sagan (1934–1996)
American Astronomer / Astrochemist / Author

To see things in the seed, that is genius.

— Lao-Tzu (6th Century B.C.)
Chinese Philosopher

The universe is full of magical things, patiently waiting for our wits to grow sharper.

— Eden Phillpotts (1862–1960)
English Author / Poet / Dramatist

Reality is nothing but a collective hunch.

— Lily Tomlin (1939–)
American Comedian / Writer / Producer

PART THREE

•

LIGHT WHIMSY

LIGHT WHIMSY

Smile-Inspiring, Fanciful Images —
Stirring Wonder

Piano-key toes

Kitten pause — in black and white

Composed silence

Delight in simultaneously seeing and
hearing from different perspectives.
Enjoy somersaulting with whimsy.

See Appendix.

Sun-sipping spring leaves
Shining with youthful zest — mature
As Empresses of Shade

Oh, the many mysteries of the evolution of shade —
and its majestic presence!

Umbrella shadows
Robust, booming, full-bodied
Sleep in — on rainy days

Being quick and agile, as well as willing and ready
at an instant's notice, fatigues devoted shadows.

Sun rays race — for dawn date
With night's dew — and gently romp
On butterfly wings

Show up; connect and reflect.
Embrace the magic; help birth miracles.

Hugs — like braided rugs

Owls' tears, ants' rears, seeds, seasons

Ovals all — ovals

Take time to be caringly silly and playful.
And immerse yourself in life's enduring, fertile cycles.

See Appendix.

To hear the heartbeat
Of a passing butterfly
Listen with your soul

Miracles abound. They twinkle into our awareness,
energized by our soul-power.

We can choose to be open to listening for
the heartbeat of a passing butterfly and be, forever,
soul-primed.

The Magic Serpent
Inhales seeds of doubt — and exhales
Bubble-borne blossoms

Heaven-sent Magic is all around us — everywhere
— in everything.

When it is not working on special assignments,
Magic enjoys itself sliding down sun rays, free-falling
in raindrops, bouncing on airborne notes of songbirds,
and warming itself in babies' breath.

Leaking into forests
Light drips from leaves — slides along limbs
Birthing — hues and textures

Colors of fading rainbows never really disappear. They flow into a thousand mornings on streams of blissful light, awakening and adorning form. Mother Earth's hues and textures are born again and again as grooved tree bark, cushy green moss, slippery-seamed tree leaves, smooth acorns with gnarly hats, and sparkly ripples rushing downstream.

Hear marsh grasses sigh
After day's dulcet dancing
With bay-breeze beaus

Marsh grasses, anticipating the ebbing of the tide,
stand tall — wildly free to greet and sway with
bay breezes. When the tide slowly flows back in,
the exhausted, dance-spent reeds ease into their
water beds to rest with sweet dreams.

May we fully embrace life's timely dance
and become empowered with tide-like rhythm to
anticipate, accept, and benefit from life's ebb and
flow.

Shadow-hidden Spirits
Birthed with wind-swept sunlight
Recede — tee-heeing

Sometimes, we may disturb Nature Spirits who are resting under a cover of darkness or in a shady spot. Occasionally, they may be startled, but usually they are delighted by chance encounters.

Softly humming while in the forest alerts nearby Nature Spirits that you are passing through. It is their custom to help visitors on their way without revealing themselves. Nonetheless, you may experience an unexplained sensation of well-being come over you.

Dream-players leave tracks
Tingling — mind-heart imprints
Awakening insights

Do you ever feel upon awakening from sleep that a troupe of players has used your head and heart as a stage?

It is said that the Wise Ones script customized dream-play designed to deliver special messages. Casting, however, requires that the chosen dreamer hop onto the stage and play one or more role.

Nevertheless, upon awaking you are the only one at the cast party — embracing a celebratory bouquet of newfound wisdom.

See Appendix.

My cat, the optimist

Waiting at night — in the spot

Where day's sun alights

And in a moment of sheer delight and wonder, I asked my beloved Bently cat, "Where have you been all my life?"

The answer filled me with even more wonder as I felt the reply, "I've been a seed flowing in a stream toward you for generations — disguised in howls and yowls and purrs — and here I am."

Hear Mother Earth hum
With hibernating chipmunks'
Soft breathing and — dreams

In early spring, Mother Earth hums with slumbering life.

Rest a hand gently on the ground and feel the vibrations of bold daffodil bulbs, snoozing chipmunks, and robust oak roots — all anticipating an awakening.

Let the imperceptible tickle your sense of wonderment.

Be a Magic-Maker
Wand away weary, worn ways
Marvel at might

And marvel at the "might-be's" — and bond with the possibilities.

Early some morning, just before the sun is about to wake up and rise, go outside. Hold up one arm with outstretched fingers toward the spot where the sun is likely to appear — and watch its rays rise slowly from your fingertips.

Willing Wind Wizard
Knowingly — whirls with gusto
Whispering wisdom

The silver-haired Wind Wizard pursues wisdom
and discerningly imparts it to those deserving.
Stay open to listening for the "knowings" in the
wind. On a breezy day, you may suddenly feel an
unexpected calmness in your heart and sense a
whispering close by — meant only for you.

Setting sun rays slide

Down spider web strands — to rest

On cushy moss beds

Sunbeams travel a long, long way to show up each morning bringing light and warmth to Mother Earth and her offspring. At the end of their workday, sun rays gracefully let go and slide into dark, comfortable places to rest.

Baroness Breeze tickles,

Tosses, and twirls young maple leaves

Playfully bossy

Be moved by the Divine Breath that caringly swirls
around you, leaving invisible calling cards saying,
"Let's stay in touch."

September sky — serene
Waits to bed her cloud-children
In sunset-blankets

The heavens smile as an ageless sky, ever-changing
clouds, and timely sun rays frolic majestically, yet
lovingly, on the horizon.

PART FOUR

•

WILLING WHIMSY

WILLING WHIMSY

Picture-Play —

Inviting the Inner Child

to Freely Romp with Wonder

Grandmother Gravity
Amused by ticklish breezes
Adjusts her leaf-cloak

Stay open to being amused, tickled, and amazed.

Swirling night wind rushes
Through dark — beyond clouds — to don
A star-covered cloak

Some nights, to get us to pay greater attention to the
heaven-sent, windswept messages whirling about —
the Wind Wizard dresses up for work.

Ocean's faithful partner
Madame Moon dips her toes
Tickling the tides

Madame Moon is flirtatious but faithful. Her sister
Grandmother Gravity is steadfast with a down-to-earth
sense of humor. Their distant cousin Baroness Breeze is
playful, yet goal-focused — whereas, the Wind Wizard
is conscientious and discerningly makes compassionate,
insightful choices.

Breeze-eased maple blossoms

Chantilly chimes, lace lyrics

Music to bees' ears

Look with delight; listen with wonder; feel the magic.

Be a blossom, a chime, a lyric.

Be a bee in the wonderland of spring.

Be — being.

Blossom-full tulip trees
Stretch heavenward — to comfort
Tired angels

One reason tulip trees grow so tall is that they have
a special, caring relationship with angels. They want
to be as close as possible to the heavens so their
blossoms are accessible as resting places, especially
when the new, inexperienced angels-in-training are
given assignments farther and farther from home.

Free, wind-borne acorns
Ardently drumbeat their touchdown
On Mother Earth's womb

As Mother Earth welcomes eager acorns carrying
oak-tree-babies-to-be, their drumming arrival sends
small, yet persistent, sensations through her belly.
These vibrations stimulate the touch-sensitive receptor
cells of specially designed soil-tillers — summoning
them to fashion earth-womb homes for the new
arrivals.

See Appendix.

Pewter-lit winter day
Snow blankets sleeping seeds
Dreaming of spring's sun

As a waning winter leaves behind a lingering blanket
of snow, various seeds may awaken from slumber
before the spring-thawing sun has arrived. Some
believe that the yawns of the awakening seeds and
bulbs generate enough warmth to help melt their
snow blankets. Crocuses are believed to have
especially warm, energetic yawns.

Suddenly springing forth
Mother Maple goes courting
Dressed in lace blossoms

As spring stirs, high-in-the-sky, elusive maple
blossoms emerge and daintily dangle alongside
newborn, soft-green leaves.

Springing from Mother Earth's womb, these
lacey blossoms journey up immense trunks to
far-reaching branch tips, where they composedly
open to their mission. Within their delicate, petite
petals are wrapped future generations of massive
maples.

Calm cloud wisps hover
Like Spirits' wind-tost white hair
Beach-walk enchantment

Clouds, being closer to the heavens, are often playgrounds for Spirits. Some lighthearted Spirits fashion their full-bodied clouds into ever-changing image-shapes — beguiling ground-bound mortals. Other more serious Spirits prefer to depict mystical imagery within their misty cloud vapors.

All that we perceive is in motion — in the now, as well as in the becoming — and can connect us with enchantment.

Crocus petals huddle
Humming warmth — fending off
Sassy snowflakes

If, during an early spring snowfall, you happen upon a
freshly opened crocus blossom, take the opportunity
to stop and listen attentively. You may hear a soft, but
defiant, humming.

It might be added that those with trained ears
report that the vibration of the humming varies
depending upon a petal's color.

Friendly dragon's heart
Sky-blue-open, ocean-deep
Mother Earth-loving

One day a large dragon was seen resting in a cloud
hovering above the ocean beach. Possibly, it had taken
a dip and was staying out of direct sunlight while drying
off. Dragons are sensitive to the sun and easily become
sunburned.

To determine whether or not a dragon is friendly,
we need only to open our hearts to the possibility.
What we are likely to find reflected back is a version of
ourselves.

Let's co-create friendly dragons.

Caterpillar tears
Touched by the Willing Wand
Become butterfly smiles

Each cocoon embracing a caterpillar has a bit of angel hair woven into it. This angelic fiber helps to promote the magic going on inside.

In time, the angel who donated the strand of hair returns to the chrysalis once or possibly twice, if necessary. On each visit she brings her Willing Wand. After unfolding it, she gently touches its golden point to her cocoon-entwined wisp of hair. With this touch her love flows into the cocoon. She then flies away — smiling.

We all possess Willing Wands.

Spring wind — be calm tonight
Bouncing tulip tree blossoms
Shelter sleeping angels

With their charming yellow-orange blossoms,
statuesquely tall tulip trees welcome Winglet Angels.
At the end of warming spring days, small Winglet
Angels fold up their wings and snuggle inside the
blossoms for much needed rest.

Winglet Angels have the honor of awakening
hibernating animals and slumbering trees, as well as
frogs and other reptiles, and all insects and seeds. At
the end of the day, the Winglets are very happy — but
very tired.

If you ever find a tulip tree blossom on the
ground, look inside. You might find the imprint
a departed Winglet Angel has recently left behind.

See Appendix.

Unborn rose blossoms
Hearing an angel sneeze
Yearn for spring's warmth

Be ever ready to connect and
respond with compassion.

A short comment about flower-petal language:

Flowers in bloom speak volumes with their beauty. Some say, however, that individual petals also speak, occasionally, among themselves while they are still encased in their buds. Those who have put their ears next to clusters of unopened buds report having heard excited, soft, little voices giggling out — "It feels as if the swarmth has arrived. Happy days; the swarmth is here!" (An accepted translation of flower-petal-speak.)

Apparently, "swarmth" is a word that waiting flower petals often use while anticipating the arrival of the necessary amount of sunshine and warm temperatures that will finally encourage their bud leaves to begin to loosen up. In the *Flower Petal Book of Words*, the term swarmth is defined as "the seasonal spring warmth that makes flower petals smile just enough to further push open their ever-protective bud leaves."

Mother Earth's timely,

Soil-scented, moist exhale

Stirs Spring Spirits

Some spirits have expertise with specific seasons. Spring Spirits rest during the winter so they are refreshed for the demands of bringing the vibrancy of spring fully alive.

Spring Spirits focus mainly on quality control and arrival schedules. Peepers are instructed on when and how loudly to peep. They are also educated regarding the reaction their peeps are likely to beget.

The more mature, experienced Spring Spirits
are given the task of counseling the newborn crocuses
to have the courage to push heavenward — even
through an early spring snow — and to keep their
spring-smiles on during their journey.

Above all else, Spring Spirits must be sure that
earthworms understand and fulfill their assignments
dutifully. But then again, earthworms are old nature-
souls and are devoted to their earthly work, so they
do not require much supervision.

Occasionally, Spring Spirits have to be firm
with young acorns eager to start their journey up
oak trunks — demanding that they be patient until
the Autumn Spirits arrive as escorts.

Morning Glory Angels
Sleepy-eyed, pollen-powdered
Unfold blooms each dawn

Vine Angels are commonly referred to as "Morning Glory Angels" because they do their early training on gentle morning glory vines.

During spring training, inexperienced Vine Angels learn how to entwine vines so that the birthing blossoms will be safe and seen. Each morning, as the vines stretch into awakening, Vine Angels sleeping among the leaves are jarred awake. Learning to swing among the climbing stems while pulling, pushing, and interweaving them takes practice.

Later in the season, the first daily task of the Vine Angels is to open the blossoms. Unfolding each petal is delicate, yet delightful, work. These angels are overjoyed to start the day working among the enchanting petals.

If you pass by a flowering morning glory vine early someday, you might be lucky enough to sense a bit of soft, blissful giggling among its blossoms.

Spring's quiet churning
Wriggle — squiggle — and squirm
Earthworm soil-toil

Earthworms are quiet and private. They are the unseen stagehands behind Mother Earth's dramatic seasonal shows. It is said that Squiggler earthworms are masters of design and direct the Wrigglers and Squirmers in what needs to be moved from here to there. They all work together to ensure that each seasonal show of blooming flowers, green grasses, and leaf-exploding trees is as dazzling as can be.

When it comes time to lay tiny cocoons holding their babies, the Squigglers, Wrigglers, and Squirmers get a bit of time off from their soil-toil, but not for long. When the baby earthworms break out of their cocoons, they become immediate and dedicated learners of worm-world work. They never cry or complain. They sense they have been selected for honorable work and anticipate making specialized contributions.

None of these earthworms has eyes, so the young Squigglers, Wrigglers, and Squirmers learn their trade by working alongside their experienced parents. It is vital to be able to identify which struggling roots and seeds need help so that they can successfully play their parts in the show. Squigglers, Wrigglers, and Squirmers learn how to effectively use special receptor cells they are born with. These receptor cells are touch-sensitive organs that feel vibrations within Mother Earth — calling them into action where they are most needed.

Impish breezes bounce
Along dawn's silver sunbeams
Tickling slumbering leaves

Early-morning breezes and sunbeams conspire to awaken snoozing leaves. These leaves house the meal-making cells, or stations, of the plant. The stations are managed by green chefs — known as "Chlorophyll Chefs." Using sunbeam stirrers as an energy source, Chlorophyll Chefs blend the appropriate amount of air-delivered carbon dioxide with ground-delivered water to produce nourishing food for the plant.

These multiple mini-food stations comprise a gigantic food chain in the plant world that is referred to by the trade name "Photosynthesis." This food chain specializes in vegetarian meal preparation. It is said that the Photosynthesis chain uses some of the most advanced equipment to find and use eco-friendly energy. Apparently, Chlorophyll Chefs use movable light-capturing panels that move in the direction of sunlight — and, in so doing, locate and employ the most effective sunbeam stirrers.

The Photosynthesis food-preparation process is not only innovative and eco-friendly but also altruistic. Individual meal-making stations give away a by-product of their work — oxygen — to all who pass by.

Once breakfast has been served, leaves frolic a bit with impish breezes and sun rays before returning to work. Some are even lucky enough to entice a friendly dragonfly to alight and give a quick massage.

Winds weave melodies with
Birdsong, leaf rustle, chipmunk chirp,
And child laughter

The Wind Wizard assigns blissful tasks to the beloved Zephyr Winds. Their most absorbing work is to toss around sweet, intriguing sounds — composing scores of soothing melodies. They also delight in the hands-on task of helping fledglings lift off from their nests into flight.

Occasionally, Zephyr Winds softly brush an old woman's cheek, helping her drift back to the enchantment of long-gone spring walks. And these gentle, spirited gusts especially like to play with the flowered images on little girls' dresses.

And, believe it or not — Zephyr Winds sometimes tickle our shadows just to watch us react.

PART FIVE

●

WRITE YOUR OWN

Vision is the ability to see the invisible in the visible,
as well as the visible in the invisible.

*The poet is the one who is able to keep the fresh
vision of the child alive.*
— Anaïs Nin (1903–1977)
American Author

Poetry can communicate before it is understood.
— T.S. Eliot (1888–1965)
Poet / Playwright / Literary Critic

*A poet dares be just so clear and no clearer. . . .
He unzips the veil . . . , but does not remove it.*
— E.B. White (1899–1985)
American Writer

PART FIVE • WRITE YOUR OWN
Play with Your Unique Vision

Creating Petite Picture Poems is fun, sometimes surprising, and usually heartwarming. Mental images stirred up by what we read, hear, and imagine, as well as by what we experience in our everyday lives, are vivid sources of inspiration. One way to practice writing a Petite Picture Poem is to reduce a longer written entry to key words that concisely capture its visual essence. You might try doing this with the following entry, "Child of Nature."

To maintain brevity, use a handful of power-words arranged in three lines. The format is similar to that of haiku in which the first line contains five syllables, the second line seven syllables, and the third five syllables. Any of the lines may vary one syllable more or less. Petite Picture Poems, however, are not intended to be haiku, which is an art form with specific attributes.

Being restricted to a limited number of syllables per line induces potent word selection and keeps the poems pithy. But your poems are your creations, so apply an approach that best embodies your unique vision and rename your entries as you see fit.

Child of Nature

_____

_____

_____

And the Spirits said to the Child of Nature:

If you like — wear twigs in your hair and paint with a
dandelion.
Some may wonder, but few will care.

If you like — run holding found-feathers and lift into
flight.
Some may marvel, but few will dare.

If you like — dance with the chipmunks and chatter their
   chatter.

Some may snicker, yet inwardly cheer.

If you like — drum on a pumpkin till its seeds start
   to rattle.

Some may ponder, yet not hear.

Be the twigs, the dandelion, and the feathers-in-flight.
Be chipmunk-chatter and pumpkin-seed-rattle.

And be forever — the bliss behind the doing.

Inner Knowing

_____

_____

_____

Stirred by an inner knowing, newborn birds head out
for a destination they have never seen before — their
wintering grounds. Guided by the stars or an innate
knowing passed on from their parents or floating in the
ether, some of these young spirits make the journey
without stopping. The blackpoll warbler, for example,
is a half-ounce flying-wonder, making its nonstop
migration from Canada to South America in about
three-and-one-half days — without food, water, or
rest. Upon arriving, little but skeleton and feathers
remains to caress its mighty spirit.

Be reminded to honor your inner knowing —
the voice in the dream, the lyrical note not heard
by others, the stirring intended only for you — and,
thus, be a good traveling companion for your spirit.

Fairies Atop Bubbles

_____

_____

_____

To strengthen their untrained wings for flight, very young fairies practice atop airborne bubbles. Bubble-flight lessons are an exhilarating experience but are fast-paced, because bubbles' life spans are short.

Adult fairies sometimes catch rides atop airborne bubbles for the adventure of the effortless high — ending suddenly in bubble-burst. They then delight in freefalling before spreading their wings in flight again.

Don't be surprised if someday you sense a wee bit of playfulness near where an escaped dish detergent bubble has burst in your kitchen.

Rose Petal Heartbeats

_____

_____

_____

Oh, the many heartbeats of a rose petal — a dutiful seed, a proud stem, a releasing bud, protective thorns, tilling earthworms, dedicated sun rays, blissful raindrops, an admiring gardener — and the Divine Creator.

Love-Ripple

_____

_____

_____

A fleeting touch of kindness to a tiny bird in distress takes flight as a potent, pristine love-ripple soaring throughout the Universe.

Best Friends

_____

_____

_____

Best friends are the bud petals on each other's blossom
— knowing when to hold tight — and when to
release.

Touch

_____

_____

_____

Touch a solid, smooth rock, and in so doing — touch
the flexible softness of the water that for so long
befriended it.

Brush Stroke

_____

_____

_____

And in the beginning, the Master created each species
with a loving brush stroke.

Others' Tears

_____

_____

_____

Others' tears may — from time to time — find their
way into our own eyes.

Butterfly Memories

_____

_____

_____

One does wonder what memories a new butterfly wakes up with.

Question Mark

_____

_____

_____

Within the rounding curves of a question mark —
slides anticipation.

Sunsets

_____

_____

_____

Sunsets, snuggling Mother Earth, perpetually slide into sunrises in the beyond.

Journey-Dots

_____

_____

_____

Life's journey-dots are so often connected with the red
fluid-flow of life's teaching-thorns.

Reaches Afar

_____

_____

_____

Laughter is an easy-to-use personal shock absorber.
It is the face-embracing, unobtrusive smile, however,
that reaches afar — both within and beyond.

Practice Being

_____

_____

_____

Practice being a genius of vision, and thus, be
connected evermore to all that is.

See the earthworm in the rose, the rainbow
in the raindrop, the moon in the turning tides,
the inspiring leader in the infant's tear, the . . .

The Same Breath

_____

_____

_____

All things share the same breath — the beast, the tree, the man . . . the air shares its spirit with all the life it supports.

— Chief Seattle (1786–1866)
Duwamish Tribe

See Appendix.

Connect

_____

_____

_____

In today's ground-bound acorn-drumming can be heard tomorrow's oak-leaf rustle, chipmunk chirps, and deer heartbeats.

To connect with the present — is to connect with the eternal.

Shift-Sprinkle

At twilight and dawn, light and dark acquiesce to each other.

It is believed that Gomoni Angels have the task of creating twilight, as well as the soft first light of dawn, by using a weighty, intoxicating stardust known as "Shift-Sprinkle." When it is scattered about at the end of the day, semi-shrouded, yet reflective, sun rays especially enjoy frolicking.

On occasion, as Gomoni Angels sweep away Shift-Sprinkle at dawn, a woozy version of "Good Morning" — sounding like "Gomoni" — can be heard. And, thus, the name "Gomoni Angels."

Angels' Wing Prints

_____

_____

_____

Snow Angels train intensively in cut-and-design
techniques. Each snowflake is crafted by a certified
Snow Angel and has her distinctive wing print
impressed upon it. To verify a snowflake's origin,
look for its wing print.

Sometimes, you can find recycled snowflakes
in icicles, but it is far more difficult to detect their
verifying wing prints.

Occasionally, blizzards occur when Snow Angels
become super-spirited and start to compete. Blizzard
flakes often lack the verifying wing print due to haste.
Nonetheless, it is always fun to look for that personal
touch.

Playing

_____

_____

_____

Shed some shadow; shake off some dust; unravel a tangle. Move more and more lightly into each moment. Arriving — always arriving.

Let's recommit to the joyful endeavor of being — and becoming. And when asked — "What are you doing?" — let's respond as we did as children: "We're playing."

Notes

Notes

Notes

APPPENDIX

PART ONE • LIFE SNIPPETS

Sacred Meeting Places   Page 6
In this context, *duality* is referring to the hypothesis that everything has a complementary opposite.

Sea of Denial   Page 11
Do you see *current* as time or as flow or as both simultaneously?

Young Belles   Page 16
Play with the words:
Chiclet / Chiclets = brand of sweet-smelling, candy-coated
    chewing gum
chicklet = slang for an attractive girl or young woman
air = space, atmosphere / manner, appearance
scents = aroma / *sense* = good judgment

Uneven Dress Hem   Page 23
stitches = sew / fasten / shooting pain
fabric = composition / components / framework / essence

Plaid-Proper Lady   Page 25
plaid = checkered / checked / check
checked / check = make sure / restrain / inhibit

Her Textured Face   Page 29
warp = threads extending lengthwise on a loom
to warp = to distort
woof (also called *weft*) = threads woven crosswise through
    the warp threads
woof may imply celebration

Her Textured Face   Page 29 (continued)
hue = shade / type / manner
texture = feel of / sense of (to touch, to mind, to heart)
fiber = thread / character, integrity / strength, courage

Years of Tears   Page 30
cataracts = clouding of lens of eye / waterfall
Play with words within the poem, and try substituting
other combinations, such as "bursting the clouded lens,"
waterfalls of denial," and so on.

Sand-Grain Cousins   Page 55
forebears = ancestors
to forbear = to have patience, to refrain, to endure —
    but *forbear* is also a variation of *forebear*. The word
    forbearers is used to mean those who came before,
    implying they were rock-solid.

PART TWO • LIGHT LIFE SNIPPETS

Bent Wisp   Page 67
wisp = something slight or fleeting / a small person
cardinal = essential, serious, key / adjective for red

PART THREE • LIGHT WHIMSY

Piano-Key Toes   Page 119
Do you see *pause* or *paws* — or both?
Is *composed* referring to a musical score or to a visual
composition such as a black-and-white photograph? And
can you switch from one visual to the other — and, thus,
change your perception?

Hugs   Page 123

Earth's elliptical orbit around the sun, as well as the tilt of earth's axis, determine when our four seasons begin and end. Presently, both spring and summer are about four days longer than either autumn or winter. In its yearly orbit around the sun, the earth travels at a speed of approximately 67,000 miles per hour.

Dream-Players Leave Tracks   Page 129

If you awaken while dreaming and you want to try to retrieve a dream that has just slipped from your consciousness, try imitating the state of REM sleep. Lie still and rapidly move your closed eyes back and forth in an attempt to stimulate your brain to recall the dream.

PART FOUR • WILLING WHIMSY

Wind-Borne Acorns   Page 144

For more information on soil-tillers with touch-sensitive receptor cells, see "Spring's Quiet Churning" on pages 158–159.

Spring Wind   Page 151

Often referred to as the yellow poplar, the tall American tulip tree is actually a member of the magnolia family.

PART FIVE • WRITE YOUR OWN

The Same Breath   Page 182

The Duwamish is a Native American tribe living in the Seattle area of Washington since the end of the last glacial period — 10,000 years ago.

Give

PETITE PICTURE POEMS
Snippets of Life and Whimsy

To Those You Love

Mail this Form with Check or Money Order to:

PowerWise Books, LLC
P.O. Box 162, Putnam Valley, NY 10579

_____ Number of Copies x $16.00   = _____

(NY Residents – Sales Tax)   = _____

Shipping / Handling for 1 Book is $4.95   = _____

Include $1.95 for Each Additional Book   = _____

Total = _____

Ship to:

Name _____

Address _____

City _____ State ____ Zip _____

Fax _____ E-mail _____

PowerWise Books

Weaving Wisdom into Power

•

As Well as Weaving:

Joy

Wonder

Open-Heartedness

and

Many-Eyed Vision